101 Things I Learned in Fashion School

Other books in the 101 Things I Learned® series

101 Things I Learned in Advertising School
101 Things I Learned in Architecture School (MIT Press)
101 Things I Learned in Business School, Second Edition
101 Things I Learned in Culinary School, Second Edition
101 Things I Learned in Engineering School
101 Things I Learned in Film School
101 Things I Learned in Law School
101 Things I Learned in Product Design School
101 Things I Learned in Urban Design School

101 Things I Learned® in Fashion School

Alfredo Cabrera with Matthew Frederick

Illustrations by Matthew Frederick and Taylor Forrest

CROWN
NEW YORK

Originally published in the United States in slightly different form by Grand Central Publishing Group, a division of Hachette Book Group, New York, in 2010.

Library of Congress Cataloging-in-Publication Data
Names: Cabrera, Alfredo. | Frederick, Matthew, author.
Title: 101 things I learned in fashion school / by Alfredo Cabrera with Matthew Frederick.
Other titles: One hundred and one things I learned in fashion school
Description: First Crown edition. | New York: Crown, an imprint of Random House, a division of Penguin Random House LLC, [2021] | Series: 101 things I learned | Includes index.
Identifiers: LCCN 2021011982 (print) | LCCN 2021011983 (ebook) | ISBN 9781524761981 (hardcover) | ISBN 9781524761998 (ebook)
Subjects: LCSH: Clothing and dress—Study and teaching. | Fashion design—Study and teaching.
Classification: LCC TT508 .C32 2021 (print) | LCC TT508 (ebook) | DDC 746.9/2076—dc23
LC record available at https://lccn.loc.gov/2021011982
LC ebook record available at https://lccn.loc.gov/2021011983

Printed in China

crownpublishing.com

Illustrations by Matthew Frederick and Taylor Forrest
Cover illustration by Matthew Frederick

9 8 7 6 5 4 3 2 1

First Crown Edition

Acknowledgments

From Alfredo

Thanks to Karin Yngvesdotter, Michele Wesen-Bryant, Howard Davis, Joseph Sullivan, and Evelyn Lontok-Capistrano for their help, guidance, advice, and support.

From Matt

Thanks to David Blaisdell, Sorche Fairbank, Taylor Forrest, Sarah Handler, Karyn Polewaczyk, Megan Ross, and Suzanne Spellen.

Author's Note

A good fashion design curriculum encourages students to come up with informed, creative solutions to the problem of dressing people for their lives. In my years of teaching, I have found that the greatest obstacle to this goal is not the acquiring of technical proficiency or adequate intellectual information—with the availability of information today, the average eight-year-old is likely more sophisticated and fashion-savvy than ever—but with accepting the need to design for real people.

The perception on the part of many students (and sometimes instructors) is that reality—real customers with real needs, real fabrics that must be constructed into real garments—is the enemy of creativity. Real experience, it is feared, means drudgery, compromise, and mediocrity. The result is that most curricula tend toward the theoretical, with practical application addressed only to the extent it is considered unavoidable. Students' designs often seem to resemble ideas more than clothing.

It took me years as a working designer to accept the importance of identifying a real living customer and recognizing what he or she will and won't wear. Far from being anti-creative, this *real*ization was for me the beginning of true creativity. For what is creativity if it isn't to take something existing in one's head and give it relevance in the real world?

The central purpose of this book, then, isn't to impart technical proficiency (although we hopefully will do some of that) or to challenge students creatively (though I hope to do that too), but to give readers some ways to connect the two. I hope to provide students with small reminders, touchstones, and catalysts to help them solve real problems creatively, and creative problems realistically.

I hope that students and designers will keep this little book handy while researching, designing, swatching, and illustrating. I hope the history lessons help readers understand that innovation happens in context and through reaction to what came before; that the lessons in organization motivate the development of a holistic design process; that the lessons in illustration demonstrate the importance of communication; and that the business lessons lend a sense of the designer's role in the larger world.

Alfredo Cabrera

101 Things I Learned in Fashion School

Fashion was born in the 12th century.

There are two ways to clothe the human form. In **draping,** simple pieces of cloth are wrapped around the body, with the excess falling in natural folds. This was the earliest method of making clothing from textiles. **Tailoring** dates to the Early European Renaissance of the 12th century, when a celebration of the natural world in science, philosophy, and art also brought about a focus on the human form. The draped robe was divided into multiple pieces that more closely fit the body. Over time, these pieces led to the making of **patterns**—templates for creating multiple, consistent garments. The advent of tailoring was thus the birth of fashion.

Draped garments are common today, but they almost always have a tailored understructure. Traditional draped clothing was ephemeral—it lost its shape when not in contact with the body.

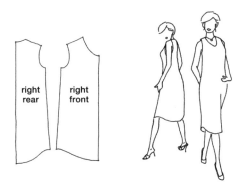

right
rear

right
front

Pattern for a sleeveless dress

Fashion-ese

collection: *n*. 1. a thematically cohesive group of garments created by a designer for a season. 2. a category of clothing, e.g., an outerwear or swimwear collection.

drape: 1. *n*. the reaction of a fabric to gravity, how it "falls." 2. *v*. to manipulate a fabric on a dress form while creating a design.

fabric story: *n*. a group of fabric samples conveying a designer's selections for a collection. Sometimes referred to as a fabric storyboard or a fabrication.

finish: *n*. 1. the surface texture of a woven fabric. 2. a final fashion drawing.

fit: 1. *n*. the way a garment drapes or falls on the body. 2. *v*. to make adjustments to a muslin or garment sample on a model or mannequin.

line: *n*. 1. the general silhouette or flow of a garment, e.g., "the line of an evening gown." 2. a synonym for collection, e.g., "our fall line emphasizes a retro look."

muslin: *n*. 1. an inexpensive, finely woven cotton fabric. 2. a prototype garment, created to refine design and fit; called a muslin regardless of the fabric.

pattern: *n*. 1. a template for the individual pieces of a garment, from which multiple examples of the garment are made. 2. a visual design, e.g., a check, stripe, or floral pattern.

Who does what

fashion designer: conceives, designs, and directs the creation of a fashion collection or fashion category.

production manager: creates costing and logistical plans for a fashion house or design firm.

patternmaker: determines the exact two-dimensional shapes of fabric needed to make a design realizable as a three-dimensional garment.

cutter: cuts fabric in the shapes determined by the patternmaker; works in a fashion house or factory.

sample-hand: constructs the first sample of a garment for the designer. Sample-hands include tailors, sewers, knitters, and embroiderers. Workers who fill two or more of these roles are called sample-makers.

machine operator: a factory sewer (although never a sample-hand); in a past era, "seamstress" referred to a female machine operator.

buyer: an employee of a retail store or chain who selects the apparel it will sell.

fashion editor: creates themes for photo shoots in the media and selects styles from various designers to illustrate those themes.

influencer: affects popular opinion, aesthetics, and purchasing patterns through social media. May or may not have a formal position in the fashion industry.

A fashion designer creates collections, not simply individual garments.

A fashion **collection** typically has from 12 to 400 garments. A designer plans a collection so that each item complements the others; they can be worn together or individually.

Attention must be given to every piece in a collection, including underpinnings and layering pieces, not just the exciting gowns, suits, dresses, and other major items. After you've worked hard to cultivate a customer for the primary garments, why send him or her elsewhere for the rest of the outfit?

Diane von Furstenberg's wrap dress

Fashion is driven by insights.

A single dress or T-shirt can be created without an underlying idea, but a successful fashion collection is driven by a concept that transcends fashion and is based on an insight into life, art, beauty, society, politics, or self. Examples of popular idea-driven fashions include:

Diane von Furstenberg's wrap dress was motivated and preceded by the broad-based entry of women into professional workplaces and a desire to project authority while remaining feminine and sexy.

Giorgio Armani's relaxed, elegant tailoring responded to the emergence of informal business models in the 1970s and 1980s and paved the way for the now-familiar "casual Friday."

Grunge, before it became a popular fashion look, was a movement that rejected lifestyle consciousness.

Athleisure reflects long-standing cultural trends toward greater informality, which are tied to postmodernism's rejection of authority and objective knowledge.

Garment designed by Yohji Yamamoto

Conceptual design began at Hiroshima.

Prior to the advent of conceptual design, the boundaries of fashion were widely agreed upon, as they were driven by conventional material, market, and cultural realities. Three Japanese designers—Rei Kawakubo, Issey Miyake, and Yohji Yamamoto—grew up in the wake of the atomic bombs dropped on Hiroshima and Nagasaki by the United States in World War II, and broke with this tradition by deliberately confronting fashion's accepted limits. Together they became the avant-garde of the late 1970s and early 1980s. They profoundly altered prevailing notions of beauty and paved the way for the end of Western hegemony in fashion.

"Art produces ugly things which frequently become beautiful with time. Fashion, on the other hand, produces beautiful things which always become ugly with time."

—JEAN COCTEAU

1   2   3   4   5

The Five C's of good pre-design

The fashion design process is complex and iterative and does not proceed in exactly the same way for all designers. Nevertheless, a general progression of pre-design steps is found in the processes of all successful designers:

1   **Customer:** Determine who you are designing for.

2   **Climate:** Define the season of the year for which the collection is intended.

3   **Concept:** Explore and create a "big idea" to inspire the entire collection.

4   **Color:** Determine a suitable color palette.

5   **Cloth:** Investigate and identify the fabrics for the garments in the collection.

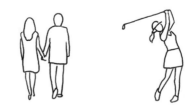

Be specific about who you *aren't* designing for.

A fashion designer must know much about the intended customer: How old is she? Where does she live? How does she make a living? How much does she earn? Where does she shop? What does she already wear? What is she not being offered? To what goals does she aspire? Such questions help a designer frame an intuitive box around the fashion design problem.

When a customer is particularly difficult to define, it can be helpful to define an entirely different customer—one for whom the product is absolutely not intended. The effort involved in assessing the lifestyle needs of an "other" usually helps a designer better grasp the intended customer.

Design outside in, top to bottom, and big to small.

The many items in a collection—suits, skirts, slacks, jackets, blouses, sweaters, accessories, and more—have to be carefully coordinated. Yet it is impossible to conceive and design everything at once. How can a designer prioritize?

Design outside in: The design of outer garments, such as coats and jackets, should be undertaken before the design of the garments they partly conceal, such as vests, blouses, and underpinnings.

Design top to bottom: Garments near the face are inherently more important than, and should receive priority over, clothing worn lower on the body.

Design big to small: Large pieces of clothing, such as dresses, suits, and coats, should almost always be designed before shirts, blouses, vests, and knit tops.

These three strategies roughly correlate with the apportionment of the fashion dollar: customers tend to spend more on items worn outside other items, on items closer to the face, and on larger items.

Organize the fabric story.

Coat/outerwear weights: heavy fabrics for fall/winter, as well as medium-weight technical fabrics and fabrics treated for water repellence for spring/summer.

Jacket or bottom weights: medium-weight fabrics for structured garments including suits, pants, skirts, tailored dresses, and jackets not worn as outerwear.

Dress/blouse weights: lightweight, sheer, and silky fabrics for shirts, blouses, flowing dresses, skirts, gowns, and other soft garments.

Sweater weights: bulky, warm fabrics for fall/winter as well as fine, cool yarns for spring/summer.

Cut & sew knits: for underpinnings, casual dresses or gowns.

Novelty fabrics: have a characteristic that makes them ideal for special items but limited for basic use. Examples include lace, leather, fur, and PVC/vinyl.

Design *into* the fabric.

A well-conceived garment can be ruined by cutting it in the wrong cloth, as many fabrics simply will not do what a designer may want or need them to do. Silk gazar, for example, is thin and paper stiff and will not accept close tailoring or free draping. Velvet may work well in a closely tailored garment or in a permanent installation such as upholstery or curtains, but it is unsuited to movement and becomes ungainly when used in large quantities in a draped or flowing garment.

Don't wait until after creating a garment's silhouette to select the fabric. Exhaustively investigate the fabric group for the entire collection before beginning the design of any garment. Design garments *into* their fabric, not the other way around.

Cotton plant

13

Cotton is a fiber, not a fabric.

A **fiber** is a filament of raw material, the smallest essential element of a garment. It may be very long or as short as a few millimeters. Fibers are made into thread or yarn by spinning, after which they are woven or knitted into cloth.

Natural fibers are found in nature. The four basic natural fibers are silk, wool (animal fibers), cotton, and linen (vegetable fibers). Others include cashmere, alpaca, vicuña, ramie, and hemp, all of which can be costly and difficult to use compared to the basic fibers.

Manufactured fibers are created by processing cellulose—the same basic material as cotton and linen. Examples include rayon, acetate, and modal.

Synthetic fibers are created by forcing a liquid chemical through a small hole to produce a continuous strand or filament. Common synthetics are nylon, polyester, and acrylic.

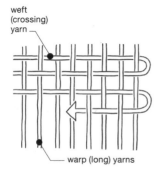

weft
(crossing)
yarn

warp (long) yarns

Weaving

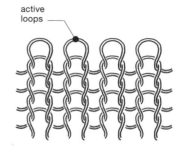

active
loops

Knitting

14

Weaving and knitting

Woven fabrics are made on a loom by repeatedly interlacing a continuous yarn through a series of parallel yarns. The parallel (**warp**) yarns are held stationary, and a crossing (**weft**) yarn is laced through them in an over-under manner.

Knitted fabrics are made from a single continuous yarn interlocked onto itself. A row of active loops (called **stitches**) is held in place by a needle as another series of loops is pulled through it with a second needle. This produces a new row of active stitches, and the process is repeated.

Nonwoven fabrics are made by mechanically, chemically, or thermally bonding fibers or threads. They are usually much weaker than woven or knitted fabrics and have limited use in fashion design. Examples include felt, netting, and polyvinyl chloride (PVC).

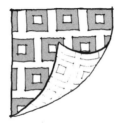

printed   yarn-dyed (woven)

Visual patterns

15

Yarn-dyed patterns are made by weaving or knitting different color yarns into a fabric. The pattern shows on both the face and reverse. Plaid, check, stripe, floral, mottled, and abstract geometrics are common examples.

Printed patterns are applied to an already woven or knitted fabric using various dye and ink processes including flatbed, rotary, transfer, discharge, and silk-screening. A printed pattern is visible on the face of a fabric, but only partially or not at all on the reverse.

Patterns that are conventionally executed as a yarn-dyed weave, such as pin-stripes and checks, can look low-end when printed. But prints are not inherently less desirable than yarn-dyed patterns. A finely detailed floral print, for example, may use ten or more colors, producing an exquisite pattern that would be virtually impossible to create in a yarn-dyed fabric.

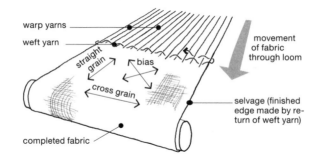

warp yarns

weft yarn

straight grain

bias

cross grain

movement of fabric through loom

selvage (finished edge made by return of weft yarn)

completed fabric

16

Straight grain is strong. Cross grain is stretchy.

Straight grain (or warp) is the long direction of woven fabric—the direction in which it moves through the loom when made. It is the stronger axis, with almost no stretch or "give." **Cross grain** (or weft) is the short direction of woven fabric, across the loom. Fabric usually has a little bit of stretch in the weft direction.

Bias is the 45-degree angle between the straight and cross grains. Fabric has the most stretch in the bias direction. Before the invention of spandex in 1959, the only way to get significant stretch from woven fabric was to cut it on the bias. This practice exists today but can be wasteful and therefore prohibitively expensive.

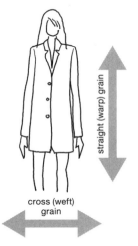

17

Cut it on the straight.

Most garment pieces should be cut on the straight—with the warp threads running vertically (perpendicular to the floor) when the wearer is standing. Because fabric stretches more in the weft direction, this helps the garment to feel a little stretchy, particularly across the back, when the wearer extends or folds her arms.

If you cut a garment other than on the straight, make sure it is for a good reason and that you are prepared for the possible trade-offs. One might, for example, cut a fabric on the cross grain to give a visual pattern the desired orientation, or on the bias to aid the draping of a full skirt. But comfort and flexibility may be compromised by the former, while the bias-cut garment may lose its shape or develop puckering at seams and hems over time.

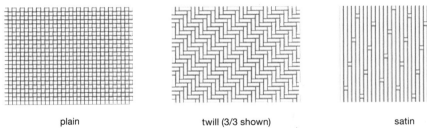

plain   twill (3/3 shown)   satin

The three most common weaves

Satin is a weave, not a surface.

The **face,** or surface, characteristic of a fabric results primarily from how it was woven. Common weaves/faces include:

18

Plain: Uses a simple, alternating, over-under pattern; wide range of fabric types.

Twill: Yarns are woven in staggered groups (e.g., three-under/three-over), producing a face with raised diagonals. Versatile and durable; suited to military uniforms, jeans, chinos, and upholstery. Includes denim, cavalry twill, and foulard (silk).

Satin: The weft yarns skip numerous warp yarns; fewer intersections result in fewer shadows and a smooth surface sheen. Includes duchesse (a stiff, glossy silk), charmeuse (a shiny, soft fabric), and peau de soie (a silk with a dull luster).

Jacquard (juh-KARD): Complexly interlaced yarns produce a subtle, shiny-matte face pattern, e.g., floral or paisley. Includes damask (tonal-patterned), brocade (multicolored), and matelassé (thick, quilt-like). Used in both home décor and clothing.

Pile: Has a surface nap above the fabric base. Produced many ways; terry cloth may be made by weaving wires into the fabric and removing them to leave behind loops of yarn. Other examples are velvet (a fine, short nap) and corduroy.

19

Fabric selection is inseparable from color selection.

When envisioning color, immediately consider the fabric. White, for example, is not an especially meaningful design option until it is associated with a fabric: note the great difference between crisp white linen and its creamy counterpart in wool. Or consider the sophistication of hot pink in high fashion peau de soie (a soft, delustered silk) versus its potentially vulgar counterpart in nylon spandex.

After a photograph by Alan Lindsay Gordon

20

Select fabrics by hand.

Color, texture, and pattern are crucial considerations in selecting fabric but are nonetheless secondary to weight, character, and hand. When browsing fabrics, try closing your eyes as you touch them to prompt clearer judgments about quality and suitability.

Always keep the bottom blade in contact with the table.

How to cut fabric

1   Never cut fabric while holding it in front of you. Rather, lay the fabric flat on a table. The table should be positioned to allow access to all sides.

2   Smooth out all creases and bubbles, using an iron as needed. Make sure the straight and cross grains are exactly perpendicular. This requires particular care with many fabrics, such as chiffon and charmeuse.

3   Mark cut lines clearly, whether making a straight or curved cut. If using a pattern or template, pin it to the fabric.

4   Use very sharp shears. Never use shears that have been used to cut paper.

5   Position yourself so you can cut perpendicular to and moving away from your body. Grip the shears firmly and cut smoothly along your lines or the edge of the pattern. Stop each cutting stroke before the blades fully close to avoid a choppy edge. Extend each cut slightly beyond the desired stopping point to ensure a clean corner where another cut meets it.

6   To cut the fabric in a different direction, do not lift or move it. Walk around the table and make the next cut from an angle similar to the previous cut.

22

An average adult is 7½ heads tall. A classic fashion figure is 9 or more heads tall.

A fashion illustration exists to represent and sell the idea behind a garment. Its design needs to appeal to the aspirations of many fashion customers: to be young, elegant, graceful, and hip. The elongated figure tends to suggest these things.

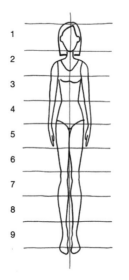

1

2

3

4

5

6

7

8

9

How to draw a 9-head tall figure

Draw a vertical line, then mark ten ticks to create nine equal segments.

1   Fill the segment with an egg or ellipse to create the head.

2   In the middle of the segment, draw the shoulders sloping downward. Total shoulder width is about 2½ times head width.

3   Locate the bust line in the upper third.

4   Draw the waist at the top of the segment, a little more than half the shoulder width. Align the elbows with the waist. Draw the hips at the bottom, about two heads wide.

5–6   Draw the crotch with a short horizontal line about ¼ of the way down Segment 5. Align the wrists with it and extend the hands to the bottom of the segment. Taper the thighs toward the bottom of Segment 6.

7–9   The tops of the knees are at the top of Segment 7. The ankles are in the middle to upper third of Segment 9.

Front and rear flats of a motorcycle jacket

Illustration types

24

Croquis (CROAK-ee): a quick working illustration depicting the general silhouette, proportions, and look of a garment. Working out the design of a garment usually takes at least three, and often many more, croquis. Most designers maintain a sketchbook for continual croquis-ing.

Blow-up: a magnified illustration of an area of a garment, used to convey details such as construction, stitching, hardware, and embellishments.

Flat: a technical illustration showing a garment laid flat and in exact proportion. It is used to communicate in detail its structure and functionality.

Finish: a fully rendered, final illustration of a fashion figure, usually 12 to 15 inches tall, communicating the attitude or sensibility of the garment or collection and the intended customer. Styling and accessories that are not necessarily part of the collection are often included.

25

Showcase the fashion, not your illustration skills.

Talented illustrators naturally want to indulge and show off. But a good artist is a self-editor who checks such impulses. He or she constantly revisits the question, "What is the minimum that will effectively communicate the idea?"

Draped fabric is nearly impossible to sketch accurately.

Tailored clothing, because it fits the body, tends to be fairly predictable and easy to portray in a two-dimensional sketch. But garments that use significant draping usually are not. Different fabrics drape in different ways and often produce a silhouette unlike what a designer intends. Patterned fabrics add further complexity, as crucial portions can disappear into folds and recesses.

When designing garments with significant draping, work directly with the fabric as you sketch to be sure you can achieve the desired final effect.

Illustration do's

Be consistent with light. Locate the light source at the top left or right, with figures in profile or ¾ view facing toward it. This will allow shadows to fall under the chin, bust, and hem and behind the arm or leg farthest from the viewer. Figures looking away from a light source may have distracting shadows on their faces.

27

Go easy on shadows. A rendering of drapery by an old master may have been beautifully modeled with heavy shadows, but a fashion rendering should be schematic and impressionistic.

Underarticulate the customer. A fashion sketch should generally communicate a prospective customer, not literally represent an actual person. Develop a repertoire of minimalist faces you can use all the time.

Minimize lines. Too many lines can lend a coloring book quality to a sketch. Use lines sparingly when emphasizing details.

Be consistent with proportions. Many illustrations of a garment or collection may be in use in a studio or office at one time. Maintain consistency of part to part and part to whole in each illustration to assist patternmakers, drapers, embroiderers, production managers, and others working on the same garment.

¾ side pose

What pose best shows it?

When deciding on a pose, consider the silhouette and details that must be communicated. The wrong pose can misrepresent a design and mislead the intended customer.

28

Figure in standing repose: Use to show off slim skirts and dressy styles. For layered ensembles, a hand on the hip reveals underpinnings. Not always best for flowing garments, which can appear wooden and heavy on a static figure.

Dynamic/walking figure: Use for flowing fabrics, garments with full silhouettes, and active or casual sport looks. Be careful when using for slim outfits; a pencil skirt on a figure with splayed legs may inadvertently suggest an A-line skirt.

Figure in profile: Most effective in showing off a dramatic silhouette, such as a full swing jacket over a pencil skirt. Also use for displaying special side detailing.

Back (rear) figures: Use only for showing important back details.

Michelangelo's *David*

Low shoulder, high hip.

29

When drawing a figure, first draw the head, then a vertical plumb line down the page, and then the intended location of the feet. The desired weight distribution of the figure determines the location of the feet relative to the plumb line. If a figure's weight is evenly distributed (static figure), the feet are spaced equally on both sides. If the weight is entirely on one leg, that leg and foot will be exactly on the plumb line, with the other off to the side. If both feet are on the same side of the plumb line the figure will appear to be falling.

In **contrapposto,** the figure is rendered with all weight on one foot and the shoulders and arms twisted slightly off-axis from the hips and legs. The side of the body with the lower shoulder will have the higher hip.

30

Skin is translucent.

Skin is not opaque; light can pass through it. When illustrating the human figure, whether using material or digital media, allow some of the page to show through to keep your figures from looking lifeless, doll-like, or cartoonish.

Counterpoint clothing color with hair and skin color.

For best effect in illustration, try pairing:

- darker clothes with fair skin and light clothes with darker skin
- a green fashion palette with red or reddish-brown hair
- a red fashion palette with black or blond hair
- a yellow fashion palette with black, brown, or red hair
- a blue fashion palette with any color hair. However, dark hair will lend elegance and sophistication to baby blue, while blond hair will soften the potential severity of navy blue by suggesting girlishness.

Avoid the firing line.

32

A tempting approach to drawing multiple figures is to align them in a row. But for a collection having a similar color palette or silhouette throughout, the result can be dull and repetitive. And a highly varied collection may appear incoherent.

Make compositions containing multiple figures dynamic. Use asymmetry and place background figures higher on the page than those in front. Group figures in twos and threes and make them aware of each other. Overlap figures, but be sure not to obscure important design features.

Render patterns generally, not literally.

33

When rendering a print or woven pattern, don't show every petal on every flower or every check in a houndstooth. Instead, envision what the pattern would look like on a model standing far enough away to appear the same size as your drawing. A drawing of a fashion figure is typically 12 to 15 inches tall; if you hold it at arm's length it will roughly match the height of a person standing 9 to 12 feet away. At this distance, you will find that tiny multicolored prints and patterns tend to merge into an overall color, while middle-scale patterns read as texture.

Step back and take a look.

When creating a garment or sketching, one works at arm's length or closer. But good designers and illustrators take frequent steps back to see how their creations look from the distances at which they are likely to be viewed by others. Designers who view their work only from working distance invariably find that their work, on presentation day, looks very different from what they expected.

Good fashion is like freestanding sculpture: interesting from every angle.

It is common to focus design effort on the front of a garment and treat the back and sides as leftovers that hold everything together. But this rarely produces a satisfactory garment.

When croquis-ing or sketching, try inverting your process: begin by applying your concept to the back of the garment and design from there. New ideas for both the back and front will emerge and a more satisfying overall design will likely result. Often you will find that a center-back zipper proves unsatisfying, and a center-front zipper, unwieldy. On the sides, you might find yourself reimagining a seam as a visual transition that helps the front "reveal" the back. Or you might discover fabric placement or creative stitching that better complements the design features on the front or back of the garment.

35

What we wear is a barometer of culture.

Clothing responds to culture, although the specific ways in which it does so are impossible to predict. When the 19th Amendment granted women the right to vote, women bobbed their hair and raised their hemlines above the knee. But during the Great Depression when conservatism might have been expected, fashions became glamorous in the extreme, as embodied by Golden Age of Hollywood actresses such as Marlene Dietrich, Ginger Rogers, and Jean Harlow.

In the 1980s, when women entered the professional ranks in large numbers, shoulder pads became popular for creating stronger physical presence. Men's fashions soon began featuring their own exaggerated shoulder pads.

Designers must understand and embrace cultural phenomena; what we wear ultimately answers to forces much larger than fashion.

Women's fashions change every day. Men's fashions change every few centuries.

In the West, before the modern era, men's and women's fashions changed with similar frequency. When the Enlightenment proclaimed the equality of all men, the need for fashion to distinguish social rank was reduced. Additionally, the standardization of military uniforms meant that men no longer went to war in their own clothes, which further neutralized perceptions of social rank among soldiers. The tailored man's suit subsequently emerged as a great social leveler in the 19th century, and it has changed very little since.

The past 130 years in women's fashion

Trend/Silhouette	Era/influence	Important Designers
Hourglass	Art Nouveau	Charles Frederick Worth
No corset/hobble skirt	Asia/Suffrage	Paul Poiret
Boyish flattened curves	19th Amendment	Gabrielle "Coco" Chanel
Bias cuts	Hollywood	Madeleine Vionnet, Adrian
Broad shoulder/A-line skirt	WWII	Elsa Schiaparelli, Mainbocher
Pointed bust/full skirt	New Look	Christian Dior, Cristóbal Balenciaga
Babyish flattened curves	Youth culture	Courrèges, Mary Quant
Rich hippies	Street clothes	Yves Saint Laurent, Roy Halston
Broad shoulder/short skirt	Conspicuous consumption	Giorgio Armani, Christian Lacroix
Minimalism	Belgium/grunge	Marc Jacobs, Helmut Lang
Theater/costume	Central Saint Martins, Fin de siècle	Alexander McQueen, John Galliano
Athleisure	Postmodern informality; internet culture	Alessandro Michele, Demna Gvasalia, Yeezy

Before rock and roll, young people dressed like their parents.

In the 1960s, the baby boom, the ascension of rock and roll as a cultural phenomenon, and widespread dissatisfaction in American and Western societies helped produce a turbulent, youth-centric counterculture. Up to this point, teens and children were usually perceived—and clothed—as younger or smaller versions of their parents.

A fashion designer jump-started France's post—World War II economy.

40

After World War II, the French textile mills lay quiet due to manufacturing having shifted to the war effort. Christian Dior helped restart the textile industry by designing unusually full skirts requiring many yards of cloth. He presented radically different seasonal silhouettes that got women shopping and money flowing. But Dior's New Look was more than a marketing strategy; more significantly, it reaffirmed the femininity that was sacrificed during the war.

"Fashion is the attempt to realize art in living forms."

—SIR FRANCIS BACON

41

Complex garments:
process usually
starts here

Conventional garments:
process usually starts
here, by deriving from an
existing garment

How to turn a sketch into a prototype

Two methods are used to develop a design sketch into a three-dimensional garment. Complex garments are often created by first draping a muslin fabric over a form, then tucking, darting, and adjusting the muslin to approximate the desired fit. The muslin is then removed and refined on the table to more accurately represent the pattern pieces.

Conventional garments are often created on the table by adapting existing garment patterns. The patterns are then transferred to the muslin and refined on the dress form.

In both instances, multiple iterations are required to create a final muslin prototype. Once the prototype is set, it is fitted to a model, and after final adjustments the garment is cut in the intended fabric.

42

Give the aesthetic gesture a reason.

Even the most highly expressive fashions must answer to functional needs, including structure, fit, use, and method of manufacture. For this reason, aesthetic design moves should be viewed as opportunities to enhance purpose. When drawing exploratory lines, immediately consider how they can make the garment work better. A dramatic, asymmetrical move might be an opportunity to locate a pocket or a hardware fastening. The introduction of color blocking might suggest the structure of the garment. An uneven hem, introduced to exalt the flow of a fabric, might also be shaped to show off a contrasting lining or an interesting shoe or boot.

Aesthetic gestures justified only by "I like it" rarely turn out to be something a designer actually does like when the final garment is realized.

Turn structure into style lines and style lines into structure.

Good designers strategically place and manipulate seams—the structural elements of a garment—to maintain fit while creating interesting aesthetic effects. They work in the opposite direction, too, turning style lines into structure. When introducing a seam into a garment for aesthetic effect—perhaps to inset a contrasting fabric or emphasize the body's curves—make sure it also helps better fit the garment to the body.

Simple clothes aren't simple to design.

When superfluous design elements are eliminated from a garment, subtler considerations, such as proportion, line, and fit, become magnified. Simple fashion solutions call for a highly refined understanding of and attention to anatomy (e.g., precisely how the neckline sits in relation to the clavicle), geometry, balance, positive and negative space, and the harmony of parts to whole.

45

A-line

Circle

Straight

Peg

Full

Pleated

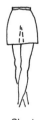

Skort

Wrap

The skirt

A-line: slight overall flare, giving it the approximate shape of the letter "A."

Circle: made from a circle of fabric with a hole in the center for the waist. Very full at the bottom, fits the waist and hips without darts or pleats. A half-circle is a variant.

Straight: hangs straight from hips to hem, the measurements of both being equal, and is fitted to the waist with a yoke (a transitional piece of fabric) or darts. Types include the pencil (mid-length) and hobble (a long skirt that hampers a full stride).

Peg: similar to a straight skirt, but the hem is smaller than the hips, so the overall shape follows the contours of the body. A trumpet skirt adds a flare at the hem.

Full: a generously sized skirt adapted to the waist by gathers or pleats. Varieties include the dirndl, pouf, and bubble.

Pleated: a full skirt with multiple creased folds of fabric that allow it to fit the waist and hips while creating an accordion or bellows effect.

Skort: a hybrid of shorts and skirt, designed to resemble a skirt.

Wrap: encircles the body with an overlap and fastener. Types include the kilt (a pleated variant) and sarong.

	Height	Weight	BMI*
Women			
U.S. (2015-16)	63.7" (161.7 cm)	170.6 lbs. (77.4kg)	29.6
Canada (2014)	64.5" (163.9 cm)	157 lbs.	26.5
Fashion model, est.	70.0" (177.8 cm)	118 lbs.	16.9
Men			
U.S. (2015-16)	69.1" (175.4 cm)	197.9 lbs. (89.8kh)	29.1
Canada (2014)	70.1" (178.1 cm)	187 lbs.	26.8
Fashion model est.	72.0" (182.9 cm)	178 lbs.	24.1

*BMI: Body Mass Index = Weight [kg] / (Height [m] x Height [m])

Age-adjusted national mean averages
Source: *National Health Statistics Reports*, 2018

Models

Body types appearing in advertisements have grown more diverse in recent years to reflect the general population. However, in the design and production areas of the fashion industry, height and size requirements remain strict, largely because preproduction garments are created in only one size.

Fit models: Used by design houses when designing garments and creating production samples. For women, typically a size 8; for men, size 40R. Models must maintain ideal size for at least two months until production fitting is completed.

Showroom models: Used when buyers from retail stores visit manufacturers and design houses to view styles for the upcoming season. They have the same sizes and measurements as fashion/editorial models.

Fashion/editorial models (magazines, advertisements, catalog, and runway): Women are 5'9" or taller, usually with measurements of 34-24-34 (size 4). Men range from 5'11" to 6'2", suit size 39 to 42 with 32" waist.

Plus-size (women) and big & tall (men) models: Found in most or all modeling categories, typically a size 14 for women, size XL/36" waist for men.

47

A good model helps a designer figure out what works.

A fitting involves many people: designers, patternmakers, sample makers, assistants, and a model. Because of the intensity of work and the need to work fluidly as a team, verbal and nonverbal shorthand is essential. A good fit model is part of the communication process. He or she understands what is needed without being asked. A hand on the hip or shoulder may mean "turn this way," while a hand on the wrist says, "lift your arm." Additionally, a good fit model will tell the designer when a garment doesn't feel right and may even be able to identify the cause of a problem and how to fix it.

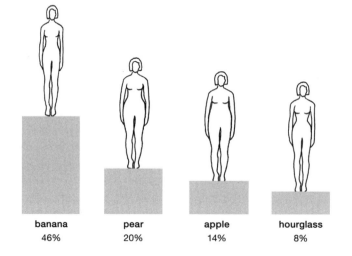

Women's body types by frequency
Source: North Carolina State University, 2005

If a garment looks good only on a 6'-tall, 120-pound model, its designer didn't do a good job.

The customers for a collection may share similarities in how they live, think, and shop, but they aren't physically homogenous. A good collection offers a variety of silhouettes, proportions, and fabrics to suit a broad range of body types.

Petites

Generally women under 5' 4". Even sizes, accompanied by a P

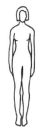

Juniors

Usually younger women who are slim in the hips and bust. Odd sizes, typically 1 to 13

Misses

Women of average height and proportion. Even sizes, typically 0 to 14

Plus sizes

Larger women. Designated by a W, e.g., 14W to 24W. Some junior collections are available in plus sizes

Grading

Designers typically design in one size—size 4 for the designer market and size 8 for the middle market. After a design is finalized, other sizes are created by adjusting key measurements, such as waist, bustline, bicep, neckline to waist, shoulder to waist, cross-chest, and front-back. Each design company uses its own **grading** formula to ensure proportional and styling consistency.

Plus and petite sizes require more fundamental proportional adjustments, and thus are not graded up or down from a size 4 or 8 but are patterned and even designed separately. This is why collections in misses are often unavailable in plus and petite sizes.

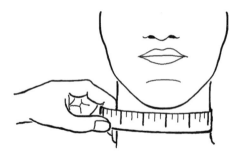

50

Take measurements with ease.

Take measurements lightly on the body or dress form, with a slight ease in the measuring tape. Important measurements include:

Bust: Take around the apex of the bust, and around the chest/under the arms. Don't follow the slope of the breasts; keep the tape horizontal all the way around.

Waist: Take around the smallest part of the torso.

Hip: Take approximately 7" below the waist, over the largest curve of the buttocks.

Neck: Take loosely enough to allow the comfortable insertion of a finger.

Other key measurements include center-front, center-back, shoulder, cross-chest, cross-back, shoulder slope, and side seam.

51

Mondrian dress by Yves Saint Laurent

Primary colors have a limited audience.

Only a few garments are ever created in straight primary (yellow, red, or blue) or secondary (orange, purple, or green) colors. A single garment in a basic color may be a great individual item, but an entire collection in basic colors will not have wide appeal. There are only a few times in a season when a customer will wear, for example, a bright yellow dress, but the same customer may wear the same dress in black, gray, or navy frequently.

Effective fashion palettes are usually based on families of color we encounter elsewhere in the everyday world: cosmetic colors, active colors, powder colors, sorbet colors, mineral colors, or earth, jewel, and spice tones.

52

Black and white are more than just black and white.

All-black or all-white palettes might seem easy, but their uniformity demands that greater attention be given to subtle considerations of texture, drape, and **hand** (the tactile feel of the fabric). Further, all blacks and all whites do not match: warm blacks (those with a brownish undertone) and cool blacks (bluish undertone) can look shabby and inexpensive when combined, and warm and cool whites can make each other look dirty. Cultural variation adds further difficulty: while bright white may show off a summer tan and creamy white may lend coziness and comfort in winter, associations of white with purity in the West and death in the East can make it an unexpectedly complicated fashion choice.

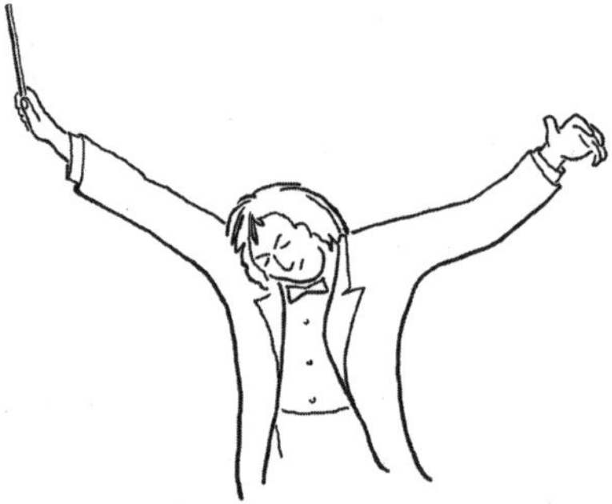

53

Two views on fashion ambition

Make big moves. Set your goals and aspirations beyond your capabilities; it's better to aim for genius and miss than aim for mediocrity and hit it. Provoke reactions. Make overly effusive design moves to see what happens. Don't do what you are already good at; try unfamiliar things to build a repertoire. Design too many garments and accessories for a collection, then scale back if necessary.

Minimize big moves. Keep big gestures to small doses. Avoid making every item in a collection a structurally or thematically complex showstopper; they will seem redundant, overdesigned, and even dull. Just as in the theater, where background characters help make a feature character more remarkable, or in the symphony where a quiet interlude separates crescendos, an aggressive fashion move should be the exception.

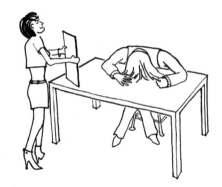

Two ways to disappoint an instructor

Do exactly what the instructor says. This tells the instructor, "I don't want to think." An instructor's design feedback isn't intended to indicate correct alternatives but to suggest a few avenues you should explore. In fact, the instructor might not mean for you to do what she suggests but may simply want to steer you away from what not to do, from a design path that is unlikely to work out. Use an instructor's suggestions to catalyze your own creative responses.

Don't do what the instructor says. This tells the instructor, "I don't want to learn." It suggests that you think you know more than her, that she wants to take over the design of your collection, or that your creations should not be subject to criticism. In fact, your instructor is trying to lend insight into a design process with which she is more experienced. Trying out alternatives that one is initially resistant to is an important part of good process.

55

Evolution of a design concept

Four design myths

Myth: Being creative means designing something that's never been seen before.
Reality: If something hasn't been seen before, it's probably not because it wasn't thought of but because it didn't work.

Myth: Shopping for ideas is copying.
Reality: Idea shopping enlarges one's mental repertoire of details, finishes, treatments, and more.

Myth: A successful final design looks like the original sketch.
Reality: A successful design concept evolves throughout the design process to best meet the customer's needs.

Myth: Reality equals banality.
Reality: Fashion must have an aspirational, emotional, or even fantastical element, but successful fashion designers dress real people.

56

It's not simply a matter of taste.

Different opinions are common in fashion, but that doesn't mean that all opinions are equal. Disagreements may sometimes be due to differences in taste, but perhaps more often they are due to differences in knowledge. The greater one's knowledge of fabric, fit, structure, color, and tailoring, the more qualified his or her fashion opinion is.

Before dismissing the contrary opinion of a critic as a matter of personal taste, ask yourself, "Who between us would be more qualified as an expert in a court of law?" Consider the possibility that in embracing the perspective of a critic, you will grow beyond both your and your critic's current understandings.

Shoe hat by Elsa Schiaparelli

"Chanel has very little taste, all of it good.
Schiaparelli has lots of taste, all of it bad."

—CRISTÓBAL BALENCIAGA

"A little bad taste is like a nice splash of paprika. We all need a splash of bad taste—it's hearty, it's healthy, it's physical. No taste is what I'm against."

—DIANA VREELAND

patch

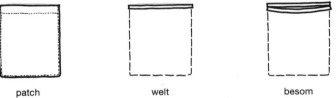

welt

besom

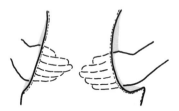

bellows
(with button flap)

kangaroo

Patch pockets imply utility. Welt and besom pockets suggest refinement.

Patch: a piece of fabric stitched onto the outside of a garment on three sides, leaving the fourth side open. Suggests functionality, in the manner of painter's or carpenter's pants, and often does not look coherent on an elegant garment.

Welt: a common pocket type, made by slitting into the fabric of the garment and hiding the pocket bag inside.

Besom: a variation on the welt, made in the manner of a large buttonhole, with the two sides of the opening finished with piping or welts.

Bellows: a variation on the patch, constructed to extend away from the garment.

Kangaroo: an informal pouch-like pocket, usually open on two sides but sometimes on the top, located on the front of the torso.

60

After a painting by Mary Cassatt

Center-back zippers are like fine crystal: best reserved for special occasions.

When one designs an interesting garment and then must determine how the wearer gets into it, a common answer is "center-back zipper." This solution is often favored by inexperienced designers because it doesn't require an invasive change to a garment.

But a back closure is only sometimes a satisfactory solution. It can be a fussy, frustrating concern when one has only fifteen minutes to dress for work. Back closures are a remnant from an era when women wore corsets and hoopskirts and had maids to truss them up in back. Today, they are more appropriate in association with major events. On her wedding day or Oscar night, after a woman has spent a lot of time and money on her hair and makeup, she is more likely to want to step into her dress than pull it over her head. A center-back zipper implies a fitting sense of occasion.

Remember hanger appeal.

Garments that are shoulderless or that have spaghetti straps or wide neck openings can be difficult to display effectively in the retail environment. An otherwise well-designed garment may look unimpressive—or worse, like a rag—on a hanger, particularly with other appealing garments nearby. Not only may the customer be unwilling to try it on; there's a good chance the store buyer won't give her a chance to do so.

Hanger loops are a simple fix for displaying a garment that won't stay on a regular hanger. However, overreliance on this solution may suggest a designer is ignoring the customer's needs: if more than perhaps 5% of a collection has this problem, the designer may be asking the customer to relentlessly exhibit too much skin.

Conan O'Brien

Random hypothesis

Your shoes say who you are; your hair or hat says how you wish to be perceived.

63

Billy Porter, motorized hat

There's a risky gray area between fashion and costume.

Fashion has traditionally served to enhance a person's real persona, while a costume transforms the wearer into a different persona. A fashion garment that tends toward the latter may be dismissed by critics as "too costumey."

But the distinction between fashion and costume is subject to much debate. It cannot be clearly delineated, and it shifts and reforms over time due to the inherent fluidity of culture. But a gray area nonetheless exists, and designers should be cognizant of the risks—and potential rewards—of entering it.

64

When designing for children, the parent is your customer.

Children can quickly ruin clothes or outgrow them in a matter of months. Because parents must frequently change diapers, clean up spills, launder, and buy replacements, practicality and cost will often outweigh all other design considerations.

65

Make children's clothing safe!

Hazards include:

- Drawstrings and cords that can cause strangulation or entrapment in a vehicle
- Toggles, cord stops, and other hardware and trim that can cause choking
- Lead and other toxins in hardware
- Flammability

66

Younger customers have bigger heads.

A younger customer is usually suggested by a larger head, slender body, long hair, and soft pink or peach makeup. Placing features slightly lower on the face also helps suggest youth. Curvy figures, short hair, graphic makeup (dark red lips, articulated lashes, and the like), and extra accessories (bracelets, necklaces) can help suggest a more mature customer.

67

The more mature, the more literal.

Generally, the more mature the customer, the more conservative, classic, and literal clothing should be; gestures toward irony, cheekiness, or costume are usually to be avoided. However, being very literal when designing for the young customer may paradoxically cross into costume, by suggesting the wearer is playing dress-up for a role beyond his or her maturity or capability.

68

Florence Griffith Joyner, track star, 1959–1998

Asymmetry implies nudity.

Symmetrical garments are common because of the natural symmetry of the human body. But asymmetry can be beautiful and provocative, in part because it suggests dressing and undressing. A symmetrical display of skin looks deliberate, secure, and final, but a single bare shoulder or arm suggests that something has fallen off—and more may yet come off.

69

Everything can't line up.

With visual patterns, matches have to be compromised at some seams in order to achieve matches in more critical areas. Give primary consideration to:

Sleeve-body match: The pattern on the bicep, one or two inches below the armhole, should match the pattern directly across on the bustline or chest.

Center seam match: The body's contours cause linear patterns to undulate. When working with plaids and vertical stripes, maintaining symmetry of vertical lines around the center seam will lend a sense of deliberateness to the pattern placement. If the pattern is multicolor, it will usually be best to place a less prominently colored stripe at the center seam.

Focal point match: On randomized print patterns, it can be cost-prohibitive, and often impossible, to achieve consistent seam matches. But some high-end designers will deliberately place a single large element in a pattern, for example a large flower or medallion, across the center-front or other prominent seam.

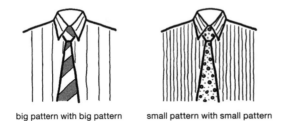

big pattern with big pattern   small pattern with small pattern   same/similar patterns

Rarely successful

small pattern with large pattern   counterpointed patterns, e.g., geometric with swirl, regularized
with randomized, segmented with continuous, etc.

Usually successful

Use counterpoints to mix patterns.

The most effective tool for harmoniously combining visual patterns is counter-point. **Scale counterpoint** groups a large pattern with a small pattern, while **type counterpoint** juxtaposes, for example, a floral pattern with a geometric pattern, a regular pattern with an irregular one, stripes with swirls, and so on.

It usually works best to counterpoint both scale and type. But if using two similar pattern types together, make sure their scales are very different. Other-wise, they are likely to confuse the eye by competing equally for its attention.

71

Bath and Bedroom in a BAG!
Sheets
Pillowcases
Curtains
Rug
Duvet
Sham
Towels
Bachelor-proof

A too-close match tends to look low-end.

A preoccupation with perfect matching—jacket to skirt, belt to shoes, or tie to pocket square—betrays a mechanical, one-to-one sensibility rather than a true aesthetic sensibility. A person of refined taste has nuanced understandings of color and pattern relationships, and can hit the right note with nonchalance and eclecticism rather than literalism.

72

Haute couture is protected by French law.

Only fashion companies judged by the Chambre de commerce et d'industrie de Paris (the Paris Chamber of Commerce) to meet specific qualifying criteria may use the label of haute couture, or "high dressmaking." A member of the Federation of Couture Houses must:

- design made-to-order clothing for private clients, with one or more fittings
- keep an atelier (design studio) in Paris and employ a minimum specified number of workers
- present a minimum specified number of original designs to the public twice each year

73

Napoleon Bonaparte (1769–1821)

Why men and women button on opposite sides

Two theories have currency: One is that men of an earlier era had to be prepared to retrieve a sword or pistol from inside their clothing at a moment's notice. A left-side-over-right-side design allowed the easiest access for the right-handed. Another theory is that proper ladies were dressed by their maids; right-over-left buttoning best accommodated a right-handed maid.

74

2-button jacket

3-button jacket

sometimes

always

never

never

Sitting, all jackets

Buttoning

The traditional man's suit

Fabric: 100% wool, cotton, or some silks. Synthetics and blends are to be avoided. Execute traditional patterns such as herringbones, windowpanes, and tweeds in gray or brown wool; pinstripes and chalk stripes in gray, navy, or black wool. Use light colors such as tan or white for cotton suits. Seersucker suits may be gray/white, navy/white, or red/white.

Jacket: Should fit closely but comfortably, with no wrinkles when buttoned. Fewer buttons elongate the torso, although only a white dinner jacket should be one-button. One or two rear vents are acceptable; a ventless jacket can look inexpensive. Shoulders should neither protrude nor be too narrow. The chest and lapels should lie flat, and the collar should lie flat against the back of the neck and show ½" of shirt collar. Sleeves should extend 1" past the wrist and allow ½" of shirt cuff to show.

Trousers: Not too roomy, but not so snug as to cause the front pockets to flare. Use pleats only with wool, one per side. The crease should break in the front between the knee and ankle. Bottoms may be cuffed or uncuffed; they should touch the shoe heel in back and the shoe upper in front.

be spat ter (be spat′ ər, bi-) *vt.* to spatter, as with soil or slander; sully

be speak (b͟ē spēk′, -bi) *vt.* **-spoke** (-spōk), **-spo ken** or **-spoke** , **-speak ing** **1** to speak for in advance; reserve **2** to be indicative of; show. From O.E. *besprecan*, "to speak about"; 1580± "to speak for, to arrange beforehand, to ask for in advance"; 1600s—1700s, "custom-made, made to order"

best (best) *adj.* [[OE *betst*]] **1** *superl. of* GOOD **2** the most excellent, suitable, desirable, etc. **3** the largest portion *[the best part of a year]* —*adv.* **1** *superl. of* WELL **2** in the highest manner —*n.* **1** the highest or

Bespoke tailoring

Bespoke tailoring is true custom tailoring. It refers to suits and shirts made to the exact specifications of the wearer, from fabric to styling to fit. It was not originally restricted to high-quality garments, but today it is the men's equivalent of haute couture and use of the term is similarly guarded by French law.

76

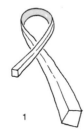

3

2

1

4

5

6

Matt knot

The collar and tie

The proportions of shirt collar, jacket lapels, and necktie are interdependent. A suit with wide lapels should usually be worn with a spread-collar shirt and a full knot, such as a Windsor, for proportional consistency. A suit with narrow lapels is usually best paired with a narrow-spread collar and a small tie knot. The tie tip should very slightly overlap the belt buckle. The most common necktie knots are:

Windsor: a classic, large, symmetrical formal knot.

Half-Windsor: a smaller, simpler version of the Windsor. Suited to medium or wide collar spreads and ties of medium weight.

Four-in-Hand: a casual, slightly asymmetrical tie knot that leaves extra tie length. Works well with narrow collar spreads and on very tall men.

Pratt: a small- to medium-sized symmetrical knot that uses less tie length than the Windsors. Starts with the reverse side facing forward.

Matt: the smallest symmetrical knot, starts reverse side forward. Good for emphasizing a tie with a prominent width and full drape.

77

"Clothes make the man. Naked people have little or no influence on society."

—MARK TWAIN

78

Sportswear isn't for sports.

Sportswear is factory-made, off-the-rack coordinated separates sold in standard sizes. It may include daywear, career, day-to-night, cocktail, casual, and evening clothes. Sportswear is the American equivalent of what the French call prêt-à-porter, or **ready-to-wear**. Clothing for athletic use is called **activewear**.

Jan	Feb	Mar	Apr	May	Jun	Jul	Aug	Sep	Oct	Nov	Dec

Mass market Winter season | Mass market Spring season | Mass market Summer season | Mass market Fall season | Mass market Winter season

Fall/winter haute couture week

Fall/winter Fashion Week

Spring/Summer designer collections begin selling at retail

Vogue Magazine spring issue

Spring/summer haute couture week

Spring/summer Fashion Week

Fall/Winter designer collections begin selling at retail

Vogue Magazine fall issue

Swimwear Fashion Week (Miami)

Fashion Week lasts four weeks.

The upper end of the fashion industry has traditionally used a two-season schedule. Twice annually, designers showcase their new collections during **Fashion Week,** which is actually four consecutive weeks. Fashion buyers and editors from around the world travel in sequence to New York, London, Milan, and Paris to preview the upcoming season at runway shows. Afterward, they visit the showrooms of designers to make their seasonal selections or schedule photo shoots.

The lower end of the industry, which includes mass-market, moderate, and lifestyle brands, has traditionally used four three-month seasons, with new products delivered to stores every month. Increasingly, however, merchandisers use a seasonless model, by which they change stock almost continually. High-volume, mass-market fashion stores may change their displays twice per week.

Displaying the goods

Grocery store display: Similar merchandise is displayed together. Common in large department stores, where the retail floor is generally divided into separate areas that individually contain suits, dresses, jeans, and so on.

Boutique display: Within a larger store, each designer has a boutique containing the store's purchase of the designer's seasonal collection.

Cross merchandising: The display of a range of products (shirts, shoes, accessories, etc.) in one thematic setting, perhaps according to color or trend. This may increase the perceived value of secondary items (e.g., underpinnings such as camisoles or tanks, or accessories such as scarves or bags) that might otherwise be overlooked by the shopper, by directing attention to the full complement of products needed for a particular fashion look. This method is often used by small stores where floor space is at a premium.

I'm business on top,
fun on the bottom.

Don't hassle me with
your rules, man.

I can't see, but they
make you see me.

I'm on the move.

Fashion is commentary.

Fashion is not simply nice clothing; it provides relevant commentary—on the wearer, on what others are wearing, on fashions that have come and gone, on the human body, and on the culture. This is partly why fashions are ephemeral; once the commentary provided by a fashion becomes familiar and generally understood, the dialogue moves on. It is also why, when a style is "recycled," something about it is different: the miniskirt is flounced, the trumpet skirt is paired with flats instead of heels, the narrow lapel jacket is worn with a primary color instead of a white shirt. The conversation has returned to a familiar topic, but with new things to say.

Fashion-as-commentary means it is possible to be well-dressed without being fashionable, or even poorly dressed—by the standards of some, at least—but very fashionable.

82

Jeans = sex

Blue jeans originally were equated with work: they were used by miners, prospectors, and laborers. Today the rivets, bar-tacks, and saddle stitching intended for rough wear have become design features connoting "authenticity." That jeans will show wear while remaining useful for years is part of this authenticity. This is why wear is often designed into them before they are ever worn.

The feature of jeans that enabled them to enter the realm of fashion is a unique center seam. It hugs the curves of the behind and, in men, projects the crotch forward from where it would be in a conventional trouser. Without this "must-do" feature, all the rivets, stitching, and sandblasting in the world will not make a proper pair of jeans.

T-shirt by Katharine Hamnett

"The origins of clothing are not practical. They are mystical and erotic. The primitive man in the wolf pelt was not keeping dry; he was saying, 'Look what I killed. Aren't I the best?'"

—KATHARINE HAMNETT

84

If you don't know how it will be made, you haven't designed it.

Good designers don't leave technical concerns, such as structure, seaming, hardware, patternmaking, and fabric selection, to others to figure out. Rather, the more accomplished a designer is, the more thoroughly she engages in technical matters. To deem oneself so brilliant as to be above them is, paradoxically, to relegate oneself to the bottom of the creative totem. Indeed, as a concept proceeds toward becoming a real garment, it must anticipate the needs of patternmakers, sample-hands, models, and even salespersons. A savvy individual among them might dismiss the objections of a poorly informed designer by saying, "What you want can't be done." How could a technically uninformed designer argue otherwise?

85

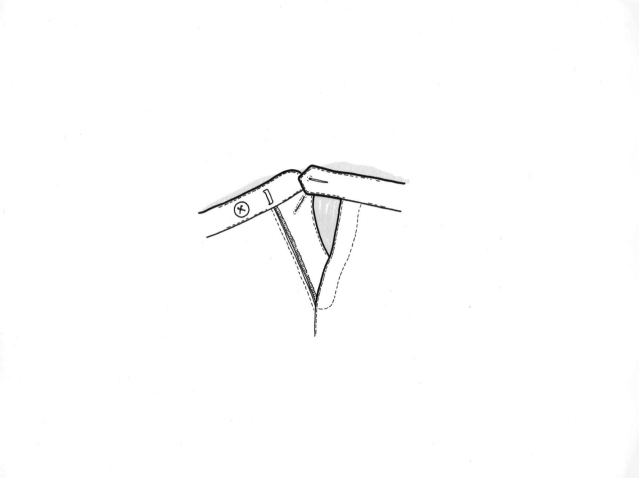

When in doubt, look in your closet.

If unsure how a garment should be constructed, look at your own wardrobe. Everyone has at least one pair of fly-front pants and a garment that buttons down the front. It doesn't take much time or effort to pull it out and replicate or adapt it.

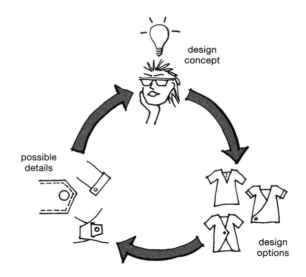

design
concept

possible
details

design
options

Details aren't add-ons.

A successful collection is conceptually driven; it is motivated and inspired by a big idea. But a big idea can rarely be understood without an awareness of details. Do blow-up drawings of garment details throughout your design process, even early on. Don't just explore decorative flourishes, but also highly functional items such as pockets, closures, and seams.

Watch for opportunities for a detail to "back-drive" the design process: you may create a garment with a specific silhouette in mind, but as the details are developed you may find that the silhouette needs to change dramatically. And occasionally, a great detail can plant the seed for an entire concept: something as simple as a fastening or cuff execution may make evident the mood or sensibility that needs to inform the entire collection.

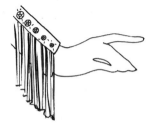

Embellishments

decorative items, including
embroidery, beading,
and trims

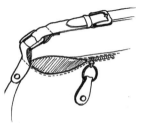

Hardware

function items, such as buttons, zippers, snaps, toggles,
rivets, and grommets

Return to the concept when executing the details.

A concept is the overall plan for a collection. It informs big decisions such as silhouette, color, and fabric selection. But it can also be the reason for a particular button, stitch, or other detail. Consider the concept to be the DNA of a collection. It is found in every aspect of it, in every garment, and in every detail.

As you work out the final details and resolution of a design, return to the concept for direction. If you find that a detail can't be executed in a way that helps the concept, it's probably telling you to rethink the concept.

88

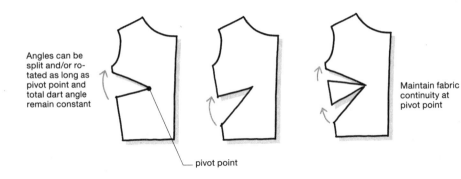

Angles can be split and/or rotated as long as pivot point and total dart angle remain constant

pivot point

Maintain fabric continuity at pivot point

3 options for a bust dart

How to pivot a dart

A dart is a fold of fabric sewn in place to accommodate the three-dimensional curvature of the body. A dart differs from a seam in that a seam joins two pieces of fabric, frequently over a large area of a garment, while a dart provides local adjustment to one piece of fabric. Darts are used much more in women's clothing than in men's, particularly to accommodate the bust.

A single dart can be divided into two or more smaller darts, pleats, tucks, gathers, etc., as long as their combined angles equal the total dart-control angle.

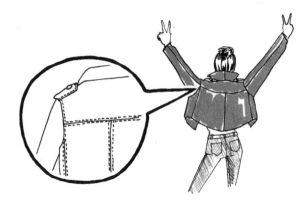

Leather doesn't come in continuous yardage.

Because leather is the skin of an animal, it isn't available in very large pieces. Consequently, a leather garment usually has more seams than the equivalent garment in fabric. Further, the finer the leather, the smaller the pieces tend to be.

Because piecing and seams are so crucial—and because leather shows off stitching beautifully—leather garments are frequently designed in a way that emphasizes and celebrates their details.

The mirror is your best friend.

A true friend, perhaps unlike a colleague or classmate, is always honest and forthright, with no agendas or ulterior motives. Looking at one's work in a mirror is like finding a new best friend: it will show you something you didn't notice before. A figure you thought was standing firmly on the page might appear to be falling over. A flat you thought perfectly symmetrical appears uneven; a muslin you believed beautifully draped is puckering and pulling; a neckline you thought flattering makes the bustline look too low.

Anticipate, but don't rely on, styling.

Styling is the arranging of garments and accessories on a model, mannequin, or display to project an overall look, persona, or attitude. A stylist does not have to be able to design, but a designer must understand styling. By frequently sketching complete head-to-toe looks that include all accessories—hats, hair, makeup, jewelry, facial hair, shoes, boots, socks, belts, gloves, etc.—a designer will be better able to maintain proportion among parts and whole, and to have each inform the other. As well, a break from focusing on clothes will often free up a designer's creative process.

While styling is critical, don't rely on it to pull off a fashion design. If you find yourself strongly intending to have a specific accessory go with a garment you are designing, there is a good chance it is because you need to incorporate the accessory's aesthetic sensibility directly into the garment.

92

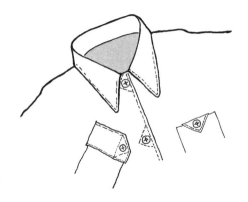

Added value

Fashion customers often need to be convinced to buy a new garment that, in effect, they already own. How does a designer sell a basic sweater or skirt to a customer who doesn't really need it?

Added value details can help reach the hesitant buyer, particularly in the middle, lower, and casual segments of the fashion market. Added value details are inherently necessary to a garment but are executed in a novel or interesting way that doesn't add significant cost. Common examples include unique buttons, special stitching, interestingly shaped pockets, and contrasting linings.

The dressmaker

Before ready-to-wear clothing, women either made their own clothes or had them made by dressmakers. Dressmakers did not design wholly new fashions but copied or adjusted the fashions of the day. Often, they added flourishes such as ruffles, flounces, covered buttons, spaghetti straps, and ribbon trims.

Today, such highly feminized, applied details are still referred to as dressmaker details, even if not created by a professional dressmaker. Dressmaker detailing is important in fashion design, although the term is sometimes used derogatorily to describe a garment in which the designer's attention was directed to flourishes and appliqué rather than to more essential considerations of silhouette, fit, line, and tailoring.

94

"Free" accessories reduce quality.

When belts, suspenders, scarves, jewelry, or other adornments are attached to a garment, their additional cost requires compensation. Consequently, such attachments are usually of low quality, cheapening what otherwise might have been an attractive item, or the garment itself will be of lower quality than its unadorned counterparts. The impulse to include an accessory with a garment usually indicates a desire to use outside elements to validate a weak design.

95

You can't increase value where it doesn't already exist.

It is almost always better to over-conceptualize a garment or collection with design moves that are overly effusive, and later have to "water it down," than belatedly attempt to augment a middling design concept that lacks true inspiration.

96

"The commonplace may be understood as a reduction of the exceptional, but the exceptional cannot be understood by amplifying the commonplace."

—EDGAR WIND (1900–1971), in *Pagan Mysteries in the Renaissance*

97

If you feel like a misunderstood genius, it might be because you're not a genius.

Even if you are a genius, the fault for being misunderstood is yours, as is the responsibility for becoming understood: you need to get better at communicating your ideas to the world.

98

Be visionary and practical.

A fashion designer must be able to conceive an entire clothing collection twelve months in advance of a fashion season. This requires an ability to holistically assess broad cultural developments, fashion trends, evolving customer needs, budgets, and manufacturing and delivery processes. At the same time, a designer has to realize every item in a collection in minute detail—from its proportions and fabric to the specific color of thread and size of buttons.

Michelangelo was doing a job.

When Pope Julius II commissioned the painting of the Sistine Chapel ceiling, Michelangelo no doubt looked at the large surface broken up by many vaults, pendentives, and pilasters and feared the innumerable restrictions, boundaries, and boxes. He probably felt further limited by the demands of making the Bible understandable to a largely illiterate congregation.

It is unlikely, however, that Michelangelo complained that he didn't like the ceiling, that it wasn't his style, or that the pope didn't "get" how he worked. Instead, Michelangelo turned practical limitations into artistic opportunities, lending testament to the true nature of creativity: it best reveals itself in solving real-world problems.

100

Johnny Cash
(1932–2003)

True style is innate.

What we recognize as visual style is the surface revelation of something that exists at a deeper, authentic level. Style is not simply how things look; it's the evidence of how they are. A genuinely stylish person is not someone who has learned to look a certain way, but one who is a certain way—a way that has natural expression in visual form.

Index

Alfredo Cabrera is an award-winning fashion designer and illustrator. His clients have included Henri Bendel, Tommy Hilfiger, Polo Jeans, Express, The Limited, Girbaud, Jones New York, Nautica, FUBU, Izod, and Liz Claiborne. He is based in New York City, where he is a faculty member at the renowned Parsons Institute/ New School for Design.

Matthew Frederick is a bestselling author, instructor of design and writing, and the creator of the 101 Things I Learned® series. He lives in New York's Hudson Valley.